Affiliate Success Unleashed:

A Step-by-Step Blueprint for Beginners

Victor M. Berta

Table of contents

Chapter 1: how affiliate marketing works

Chapter 2: Choosing Your Niche

Chapter 3:Researching Profitable Affiliate Programs:

Chapter 4: Build a Platform

Chapter 5: Create Quality Content

Chapter 6: Use SEO Strategies

Chapter 7: Promote Affiliate Products

Chapter 8: Build an Email List

Chapter 9: Engage on Social Media
Chapter 10: Analyse and Optimise
Chapter 11: Stay Updated

Introduction

Welcome to "Affiliate Success Unleashed: A Step-by-Step Blueprint for Beginners," the book that will help you get the most out of affiliate marketing. This complete guide takes you on a journey designed just for beginners, giving you the tools and knowledge you need to succeed in the ever-changing world of affiliate marketing.

Looking through this book, you'll learn the basic ideas behind affiliate marketing, how to pick the right topic, about different affiliate programmes, and how to write interesting content. This step-by-step guide is meant to give newbies the tools they need to not only understand the ins and outs of affiliate marketing but also reach their full potential for success in the constantly changing digital world.

Are you ready to turn your passion into a business and start your road to becoming financially independent? You can use "Affiliate

Success Unleashed" as a help. Read the book, take in the information, and start making steps towards a steady online income.

You are ready to be a successful partner. Let's open the door for it together!

Chapter 1: How Affiliate Marketing Works

How to Understand Affiliate Marketing: A Deep Dive into the Basics

Affiliate marketing stands as a dynamic and lucrative avenue in the digital world, where individuals and businesses can form symbiotic partnerships to drive sales and generate income. At its core, affiliate marketing revolves around the simple yet powerful premise of promoting other people's goods or services and earning a commission for every sale or action facilitated through a unique affiliate link. In this study, we delve into the basic aspects of affiliate marketing, unraveling its mechanics and highlighting the key elements that define this multifaceted ecosystem.

1.Defining Affiliate Marketing: - Promoting Products for Commission:

Affiliate marketing fundamentally entails promoting products or services made by others. As an affiliate, you act as a middleman connecting consumers with the goods they might be interested in. In return for your promotional efforts, you earn a commission on each good sale or specified action.

- **Affiliate Link as the Catalyst**

At the heart of affiliate marketing is the idea of the affiliate link. This unique URL is given to affiliates by merchants and serves as the bridge between the affiliate's promotional efforts and the merchant's goods. When a consumer clicks on this affiliate link and makes a purchase or takes a desired action, the affiliate is credited with the recommendation.

2. The Affiliate Marketing Ecosystem:- Key Players:

The affiliate marketing ecosystem includes three major players: the merchant (or advertiser), the affiliate (or publisher), and the consumer. The merchant is the entity that creates or owns the goods or services, the affiliate is the marketer who promotes them, and the consumer is the end user who engages with the products through the affiliate's promotional efforts.

- Performance-Based Model:

Unlike traditional advertising models where payments are made upfront, affiliate marketing works on a performance-based model. Affiliates are compensated based on the outcomes they produce, be it a sale, click, or lead. This aligns the goals of affiliates and merchants, fostering a results-driven partnership.

3.The Role of Affiliate Links:- Tracking and Attribution:

Affiliate links are important in tracking and attributing actions to specific affiliates. When a consumer clicks on an affiliate link, a cookie is usually stored on their computer. This cookie includes information that allows the tracking system to identify the affiliate responsible for the referral, even if the purchase happens later.

- Unique Identifiers:

Each affiliate is given a unique affiliate link. This individual identifier is crucial for correctly attributing conversions to the respective affiliate. It ensures that each participant in the affiliate program gets due credit for the sales or actions generated through their promotional efforts.

4. Commission Structures: - Pay-Per-Sale (PPS):

The most popular commission structure in affiliate marketing is Pay-Per-Sale (PPS). Affiliates earn a predetermined percentage of the sale amount when a referred customer makes a purchase. This model ties the affiliate's compensation directly to the revenue produced for the merchant.

- Pay-Per-Click (PPC):

Pay-Per-Click (PPC) is another commission structure where affiliates earn based on the number of clicks their affiliate links receive, regardless of whether the referred customer makes a purchase. This model works on driving traffic to the merchant's site.

- Pay-Per-Lead (PPL):

In a Pay-Per-Lead (PPL) scheme, affiliates make a commission for generating leads for the merchant. This could involve steps such as signing up for a trial, filling out a form, or subscribing to a newsletter. PPL is particularly prevalent in businesses where capturing leads is valuable.

5. Affiliate Marketing Workflow:- Affiliate Registration:

The journey for an affiliate usually starts with the registration process. Affiliates join an affiliate scheme by signing up with a merchant. Upon approval, they gain access to resources such as affiliate links, banners, and tracking tools given by the merchant.

- **Content Creation:**

Once registered, affiliates embark on creating content to promote the merchant's goods or services. This content can take various forms, including blog posts, reviews, social media posts, videos, or email campaigns. The goal is to produce engaging and persuasive material that encourages consumer action.

- **Promotion and Distribution:**

Affiliates carefully embed their affiliate links within the created content and distribute it through various platforms. These channels could include their website, social media platforms, email newsletters, or other relevant avenues where their target audience is likely to connect.

- **Tracking and Analytics:**

The success of an affiliate's efforts is closely monitored through tracking and analytics. Sophisticated tools provide insights into key measures such as click-through rates, conversion rates, and earnings. Affiliates leverage this data to assess the success of their campaigns and make informed adjustments.

6. Benefits for Merchants: - Cost-Effective Marketing:

For merchants, affiliate marketing presents a cost-effective marketing approach. Instead of allocating set budgets to traditional advertising with uncertain returns, merchants only incur costs when affiliates deliver actual results. This performance-based method aligns with efficient resource utilisation.

- Expanded Reach:
The affiliate marketing model allows merchants to expand their reach significantly. Affiliates often possess

established followings or niche knowledge, allowing merchants to tap into diverse audiences. This diversity can lead to greater brand exposure, customer acquisition, and market penetration.

- Risk Mitigation:
The risk-sharing aspects of affiliate marketing mitigate risks for merchants. They pay for actual sales or leads, minimising the financial risks involved with traditional advertising models. This risk-sharing method fosters a mutually beneficial relationship where both parties have a vested

interest in driving successful outcomes.

7.Benefits for Affiliates: - Monetization Opportunities:

Affiliates stand to benefit from the monetization opportunities that affiliate marketing offers. This approach offers a tangible income stream, allowing affiliates to earn commissions for their promotional efforts. This can be particularly attractive for individuals or content creators wanting additional income streams.

- **Diverse Product Selection:**

Affiliates enjoy the flexibility of choosing goods or services to promote from a diverse array of options. This diversity empowers affiliates to align their promotional efforts with their interests or cater to the tastes of their audience. The ability to select goods relevant to their niche enhances the authenticity of their marketing efforts.

- **Flexibility and Autonomy:**

One of the appealing aspects for affiliates is the high degree of flexibility and autonomy provided by affiliate marketing. Affiliates can choose when and how to promote goods, pick the platforms that align with their strengths, and adapt their strategies based on performance insights. This flexibility caters to different lifestyles and preferences.

8. Challenges and Considerations: - Dependency on Merchant Practices:

Affiliates face a level of dependence on the practices of the merchants they choose to promote. Issues such as changes to commission structures, product availability, or the quality of merchant services can affect affiliates. This highlights the importance of selecting reputable merchants and keeping informed about their practices.

In essence, understanding affiliate marketing needs grasping its basic principles and the interplay between merchants, affiliates, and customers. This model's adaptability, performance-driven nature, and potential for mutually beneficial collaborations make it a cornerstone in the modern digital marketing environment. As affiliates strategically navigate this ecosystem, armed with a deep knowledge of its mechanics, they unlock a realm of possibilities for income generation and business growth.

Chapter 2: Choosing Your Niche:

A Strategic Foundation for Affiliate Success

In the expansive world of affiliate marketing, the phrase "Choose Your Niche" serves as a basic mantra, embodying the essence of strategic decision-making that can significantly impact the trajectory of one's affiliate journey. This important step involves selecting a specific market segment or area of interest that aligns with your passions or expertise. In this study, we delve into the intricacies of choosing your niche, stressing the importance of passion and knowledge as catalysts for creating compelling content and fostering genuine connections with your audience.

1. Understanding the Concept of a Niche:

- Defining a Niche:

A niche, in the context of affiliate marketing, refers to a specialised segment of the market that caters to a distinct audience with specific needs, hobbies, or preferences. Choosing a niche involves narrowing down your focus to a particular subject, business, or product category.

- **Benefits of Niche Marketing:**

Niche marketing offers several advantages over a broad, generalised method. By targeting a specific audience, you can tailor your content to address their unique requirements, establish yourself as an expert in that area, and ultimately build a more engaged and loyal audience.

2. Passion as a Guiding Force:

- The Power of Passion

Selecting a niche aligned with your interests can be a game-changer. Passion serves as a driving force that fuels your enthusiasm, creativity, and resilience in the face of difficulties. When you're truly passionate about your chosen niche, your commitment shines through in your content, resonating with your audience on a deeper level.

- Authenticity in Content Creation:
Passionate content creators have a natural tendency to produce authentic and genuine material. Whether it's in

the form of blog posts, videos, reviews, or social media interaction, authenticity is a magnet that attracts and retains an audience. Your passion becomes a beacon that draws like-minded individuals who share your excitement.

- **Sustainability and Consistency**:
Passion adds to the sustainability of your affiliate marketing venture. It sustains your interest and motivation over the long haul, avoiding burnout. When you truly love what you do, consistency becomes second nature, as you derive joy from continuously making

and sharing content within your niche.

3. Knowledge as a Competitive Edge:

- Leveraging Expertise:

Choosing a niche where you have knowledge or experience provides a competitive edge. Your expertise places you as a credible source of information, fostering trust with your audience. Whether you're delving into product reviews, providing tutorials, or offering insights, your expertise adds value to your material.

- Content Quality and Depth:

Knowledge allows you to make content with depth and substance. Instead of surface-level information, you can give in-depth analyses, comprehensive guides, and nuanced perspectives within your niche. This level of quality not only attracts a discerning audience but also establishes your authority in the chosen area.

- **Navigating Challenges Effectively:** Knowledge serves as a navigational compass, helping you handle challenges within your niche. Whether it's staying abreast of industry trends, knowing your audience's evolving needs, or adapting to changes, your knowledge base empowers you to make informed decisions and adjustments.

4. Identifying Your Passion and Knowledge:

- Self-Reflection:

Begin the process of picking your niche by engaging in self-reflection. Identify your passions, hobbies, and areas that truly excite you. Consider the things you enjoy learning about or discussing in your daily life. This introspective journey lays the basis for aligning your affiliate marketing venture with your authentic interests.

- **Assessing Expertise:** Evaluate your expertise and knowledge across different domains. What skills do you possess? In which areas do you have a deep knowledge or experience? Recognizing your strengths allows you to leverage them successfully in your chosen niche, providing valuable insights to your audience.

- **Exploring Overlapping Areas:** Explore potential niches where your passions and skills intersect. This overlap reflects the sweet spot where your authentic interest converges with your expertise. This alignment sets the stage for a compelling and sustainable affiliate marketing business.

5. Researching Market Viability:

- Market Demand:

While desire and knowledge are foundational, it's essential to assess the market demand for your chosen niche. Research the popularity and demand for goods or services within your niche. Tools like keyword research and market analysis can provide insights into the search rate and trends related to your chosen subject.

- **Competitive Landscape:** Evaluate the competitive environment within your niche. Assess the current affiliates and content creators working in the same space. Identify chances for differentiation and innovation.

Understanding the competitive dynamics helps you figure out your unique value offering.

- **Affiliate Program Availability:** Ensure that there are viable affiliate programs related to your field. Explore affiliate networks and platforms to find merchants offering related products or services. Availability of affiliate programs guarantees that you have opportunities to monetize your efforts within your chosen niche.

6. **Building Audience Connection:**

- **Targeting Your Audience:**

Choosing a niche is not only about your hobbies but also about understanding and connecting with your target audience. Identify the demographic and psychographic traits of the audience you aim to reach. Tailor your content to meet their wants, aspirations, and pain points.

- **Establishing Trust and Relatability:**
Passion and knowledge add to building trust and relatability with your audience. When you talk authentically about a subject you love and understand deeply, your audience is more likely to trust your recommendations. This trust forms the bedrock of good affiliate relationships.

- **Engagement and Community Building:**
Foster engagement within your niche by

actively participating in conversations, responding to audience questions, and building a sense of community. Building a community around your niche not only improves your content's reach but also strengthens the bonds with your audience.

7. Adaptability for Long-Term Growth:

- Future Trends and Evolution:

Consider the adaptability of your chosen area for long-term growth. Anticipate future trends and possible evolutions within the niche. A niche that allows for diversification and expansion over time positions you for sustained relevance in a dynamic digital world.

- **Personal Growth and Evolution:**

Acknowledge your own potential for growth and development within your chosen niche. As you delve deeper into your interests and grow your knowledge, your affiliate marketing strategies may evolve. Choose a niche that accommodates your personal and professional growth over the long run.

Diversification Opportunities:

Assess the possibility for diversification

within your niche. Are there complementary sub-niches or related themes that align with your overarching theme? Diversification provides avenues for growing your content portfolio and catering to a broader audience while staying true to your core interests.

8. Case Studies and Success Stories:

-Learning from Examples:

Explore case studies and success stories within the affiliate marketing environment. Analyze how great affiliates have chosen and navigated their niches. What strategies did they apply to align their passions and knowledge with market demands? Learning from examples offers valuable insights into effective niche selection.

Adapting Strategies: While case studies offer useful lessons, it's crucial to adapt strategies to your unique circumstances. Your passion, skills , and individual strengths are unique, shaping a personalised approach to niche selection and content creation. Use success stories as inspiration while tailoring your path based on your skills.

9. Conclusion:

- Strategic Foundation for Success:

In the intricate tapestry of affiliate marketing, picking your niche serves as a strategic foundation for success. The synergy between passion and knowledge pushes you toward creating authentic, high-quality content that resonates with your audience. This strategic alignment not only improves your enjoyment and sustainability in the affiliate marketing journey but also forms the cornerstone of lasting connections with your audience.

Iterative Process of Refinement:

The process of choosing your niche is not a one-time choice but an iterative journey of refinement. As you interact with your audience, monitor market trends, and evolve personally and professionally, be open to reassessing and refining your niche strategy. This adaptability ensures that you stay current and continue to thrive in the ever-evolving landscape of affiliate marketing.

- Empowering Your Affiliate Journey:

Ultimately, choosing your niche is about

empowering your affiliate journey with meaning and resonance. It's about weaving your unique hobbies, skills, and audience connecti. on into a tapestry that not only reflects who you are but also paves the way for sustained success in the dynamic and rewarding world of affiliate marketing.

Chapter 3: Researching Profitable Affiliate Programs:

A Strategic Guide for Success

Embarking on a journey in affiliate marketing requires more than just enthusiasm and content creation—it necessitates a keen understanding of the affiliate programs you choose to work with. The basis of a successful affiliate business lies in identifying and aligning yourself with reputable and profitable affiliate programs within your chosen niche. In this comprehensive guide, we explore the intricacies of researching and selecting affiliate programs strategically, emphasising the importance of reliability, commission structures, and the quality of goods or services provided.

1. **Understanding Affiliate Programs: Affiliate Program Essentials:**

An affiliate program is a structured arrangement between merchants and affiliates, facilitating the promotion of goods or services in return for a commission on successful sales, clicks, or leads. These programs provide affiliates with unique tracking links, promotional materials, and a commission structure that outlines how earnings are calculated.

- Affiliate Networks vs. In-House Programs:
Affiliate programs can be part of affiliate networks or in-house programs handled directly by merchants. Affiliate networks act as intermediaries, connecting affiliates with a multitude of businesses. In-house programs are managed exclusively by the merchant, often giving a more direct and personalised partnership.

2. Choosing Affiliate Programs in Your Niche:

-Alignment with Your Niche:

The first step in studying affiliate programs is to ensure alignment with your chosen niche. Look for programs that offer products or services related to your content and audience. This alignment improves the authenticity of your promotional efforts and increases the chance of conversions.

- **Relevance to Your Audience:**

Consider the wants and preferences of your community when selecting affiliate programs. The goods or services promoted should resonate with your audience, addressing their pain points or fulfilling their desires. This relevance strengthens the connection between your material and the affiliate offers.

-       **Diversification Opportunities:** Explore affiliate programs that allow for diversification within your field. A diverse array of goods or services provides flexibility in content creation and caters to different segments of your audience. Diversification also mitigates risks associated with changes in consumer tastes or market trends.

3. **Key Criteria for Research:**
- **Reputation of the Merchant:**
Research the name of the merchant offering the affiliate program. Choose merchants known for ethical business practices, quality goods or services, and a commitment to customer satisfaction. A reputable merchant enhances the credibility of your suggestions and builds trust with your audience.
- **Commission Structures**:
Assess the commission arrangements of affiliate programs. Different

programs may offer different commission models, such as Pay-Per-Sale (PPS), Pay-Per-Click (PPC), or Pay-Per-Lead (PPL). Evaluate the commission rates to ensure they match with your revenue goals and the perceived value of the goods or services.

- Cookie Duration:

Cookie duration refers to the timeframe during which an affiliate is credited for a connection. Longer cookie durations provide affiliates with a more extended window of opportunity for earning commissions on subsequent purchases made by the recommended customer. Consider programs with favourable cookie durations for improved earning potential.

-   **Tracking and Attribution:**
Robust tracking and attribution methods are crucial for correctly crediting affiliates for their referrals. Look for programs with reliable tracking systems that record and attribute actions to the correct affiliate. This ensures that you receive proper credit for the conversions created through your promotional efforts.

4. Research Tools and Platforms:

- Affiliate Networks: Explore reputable affiliate networks that aggregate programs across various areas. Networks like ShareASale, CJ Affiliate, and Rakuten Affiliate Marketing provide a centralized platform for finding and joining multiple affiliate programs. These networks often offer extra tools and analytics for affiliates.

- Merchant Websites: Visit the websites of individual merchants within your field. Many merchants host their affiliate programs straight on their websites. Navigate to the "Affiliate Program" or "Partner Program" section to find information about commission structures, promotional materials, and how to join.

- **Affiliate Directories**: Utilise affiliate directories or databases that collect information about affiliate programs. These directories categorise programs based on niche, making it easier for affiliates to find relevant opportunities. Examples include Affilorama and AffiliatePrograms.com.

5. Analysing Program Terms and Conditions:

- Payout Frequency and Thresholds:
Examine the payout frequency and minimum payout limits of affiliate programs. Some programs have weekly payouts, while others may have longer intervals. Ensure that the payout frequency fits with your financial goals. Additionally, check if there are minimum earning thresholds that must be reached before getting payouts.

- Restrictions and Policies:
Thoroughly review the terms and conditions of affiliate programs to find any restrictions or

policies. Pay attention to exclusions, geographical limits, and promotional methods that may be prohibited. Understanding these restrictions helps you work within the guidelines set by the merchant.

- **Affiliate Support and Resources:**

Assess the amount of support and resources given by the affiliate program. Look for programs that offer affiliates marketing materials, product information, and dedicated help. Access to tools enhances your ability to create effective promotional material and navigate challenges.

6. **Merchant Communication and Responsiveness:**

- **Communication Channels:** Evaluate the communication channels created by the merchant. Responsive merchants often have designated channels for affiliate questions, providing a means for affiliates to seek assistance or clarification. Effective communication is crucial for resolving queries and addressing concerns quickly.

- **Affiliate News and Updates:**

Check if the merchant regularly shares updates, promotions, or changes to affiliates. Merchants that keep affiliates informed about new product launches, promotional campaigns, or program improvements allow affiliates to stay proactive and align their strategies accordingly.

- **Community Engagement:**
Some merchants promote community engagement among their affiliates. This may involve discussions, social media groups, or exclusive events. Participating in such communities allows

affiliates to share
insights, seek advice,
and work with fellow
affiliates and the
merchant.

7. Quality of Products or Services:

- Product or Service Integrity:

The quality and integrity
of the products or
services given by the
merchant significantly
impact the success of
your affiliate marketing
efforts. Choose
programs where the
goods or services align
with your standards and
provide genuine value to
your audience. High-
quality offerings
improve customer
satisfaction and trust.

- Customer Reviews and Feedback:

Investigate customer reviews and feedback related to the goods or services promoted through the affiliate program. Positive reviews and testimonials indicate customer happiness and validate the legitimacy of the offerings. Conversely, negative reviews may raise concerns about the merchant's trustworthiness.

- Trial and Testing:

If feasible, consider trying the goods or services yourself before promoting them. Personal experience allows you to authentically talk about the benefits and drawbacks, adding a layer of credibility to your promotional material. Testing the offerings ensures that you confidently endorse goods or services to your audience.

8. Monitoring Program Performance:

- Analytics and Reporting:

Leverage analytics and reporting tools offered by the affiliate program or network. Analyse key data such as clicks, conversions, and earnings. Monitoring these metrics provides insights into the performance of your promotional efforts and helps spot successful strategies or areas for improvement.

- **Split Testing and Optimization:**
Implement split testing (A/B testing) to optimise your promotional tactics. Experiment with variations in your content, call-to-action elements, or promotional platforms. Analyse the results to refine your approach and focus on tactics that give higher conversions.

- **Adaptability to Changes:**
Stay informed about any changes or updates to

the affiliate scheme. Merchants may change commission structures, terms, or promotional guidelines. Adaptability allows you to proactively adjust your strategies, ensuring continued success in an evolving affiliate marketing environment.

9.   Long-Term Partnership Considerations:

-   Scalability and Growth Potential:

Assess the scalability and growth potential of the affiliate scheme. A program that accommodates your long-term goals and allows for scalability aligns with your aims for sustained success. Consider whether the program offers chances for increased earnings as your audience expands.

- **Exclusive Partnerships or Exclusivity Clauses:** Be mindful of exclusive relationships or exclusivity terms within affiliate programs. Some programs may request exclusivity, limiting your ability to promote competing goods or services. Evaluate the consequences of exclusivity clauses and ensure they fit with your overall affiliate marketing strategy.

- **Merger and Acquisition Risks:**

In the dynamic business environment, mergers or acquisitions may impact affiliate programs. Be aware of potential risks connected with changes in ownership or structural adjustments. Stay vigilant and evaluate the continuity and terms of the program in the event of major business changes.

10. Legal and Compliance Considerations:

- Affiliate Agreement Compliance:

Adhere to the terms stated in the affiliate agreement. Compliance with program guidelines, promotional methods, and ethical practices is important for maintaining a positive relationship with the merchant. Non-compliance may lead to the termination of the affiliate relationship.

- **Disclosure and Transparency:**
Practice transparency in your promotional efforts by revealing your affiliate agreements. Compliance with disclosure standards ensures ethical and transparent contact with your audience. Transparent disclosure builds trust and creates a genuine relationship with your audience.

- **Data Protection and Privacy:**

Consider data protection and privacy regulations applied to your geographic area and the merchant's operations. Adhere to privacy policies, especially if you collect and handle customer data as part of your promotional activities. Prioritise ethical and lawful data practices.

11. Case Studies and Peer Experiences:

- Learning from Case Studies:

Explore case studies and insights shared by other affiliates within your field. Learning from the experiences of peers provides valuable views on the effectiveness of specific affiliate programs, possible challenges, and successful strategies. Case studies offer practical insights that can guide your decision-making.

- **Community Forums and Discussions:** Engage with affiliate marketing group forums and discussions. Platforms like affiliate marketing subreddits, industry forums, or dedicated community spaces allow you to connect with experienced affiliates. Seek advice, ask questions, and join in discussions to gain from collective knowledge and experiences.

- **Adapting Strategies:** While case studies and peer experiences offer useful insights, it's crucial to adapt strategies to your unique circumstances. Factors such as audience demographics, material style, and promotional channels change among affiliates. Use shared experiences as learning opportunities while tailoring your approach based on your unique strengths.

12. Conclusion:

- **Strategic Affiliate Program Selection:** Researching profitable affiliate programs is a pivotal step in the strategic growth of your affiliate marketing journey. By carefully evaluating the reputation of merchants, commission structures, and the quality of goods or services, you lay the groundwork for a fruitful and enduring partnership.

- **Ongoing Evaluation and Optimization**: The process of selecting affiliate programs is not static; it requires ongoing review and optimization. Stay vigilant, adapt to changes, and optimise your tactics based on performance insights. A dynamic and informed approach guarantees that your affiliate marketing endeavours stay resilient in the ever-evolving digital landscape.

- **Empowering Your Affiliate Success**: Ultimately, the careful selection of affiliate programs strengthens your affiliate marketing success. By aligning with reputable merchants, understanding program dynamics, and prioritising the needs of your audience, you build partnerships that contribute to your reputation, financial goals, and long-term growth within the dynamic ecosystem of affiliate marketing.

Chapter 4: Build a Platform

Establishing a robust online platform is the cornerstone of a successful affiliate marketing business. Whether you're a seasoned marketer or just stepping into the world of online business, building a platform provides you with a centralised space to connect with your audience, share valuable content, and carefully integrate affiliate links. This platform serves as the nexus where your unique voice and promotional efforts converge, creating a dynamic space for audience interaction and revenue generation.

The first step in building your platform is to decide on the type of online presence that aligns with your goals and viewers. Three main options are commonly chosen by affiliate marketers: a blog, a website, or leveraging social media channels.

1. Blogging:

Blogs offer a versatile and content-centric platform, allowing you to create in-depth articles, reviews, and other written content. This method is ideal if you enjoy writing and want to provide your audience with comprehensive information about your chosen niche and the products or services you're promoting.

When starting a blog, select a user-friendly platform such as WordPress, Blogger, or Medium. These platforms offer a range of customizable templates, making it easy to build a visually appealing and user-friendly blog. Choose a domain name that shows your niche and is easy for your audience to remember.

Consistent and high-quality content is the lifeblood of a good blog. Develop a content strategy that fits with your niche and audience preferences. Consider creating a mix of evergreen content, which stays useful over time, and timely content that addresses current trends or industry updates.

Integrate your affiliate links easily within your blog content. Rather than appearing as overt promotions, these links should complement the natural flow of your pieces. Craft compelling call-to-action (CTA) statements that encourage readers to explore the goods or services you're endorsing.

Engage with your followers through comments, social media, and email. Foster a feeling of community by responding to comments, encouraging discussions, and incorporating feedback into your future content. Building a loyal readership is not only rewarding but also adds to the success of your affiliate marketing efforts.

2. Website:

A dedicated website offers a more comprehensive and

customizable platform for affiliate marketing. It offers the flexibility to incorporate various types of material, including written articles, videos, infographics, and more. This choice is suitable for those who want to curate a diverse range of content to cater to different audience preferences.

Choose a reliable web hosting service and a domain name that shows your brand and niche. Platforms like WordPress.org, Wix, and Squarespace offer powerful tools for creating and customising websites without extensive technical understanding. Organise your website logically, creating clear navigation menus that guide users to different areas, such as product reviews, blog posts, and affiliate recommendations.

Invest time in designing a visually appealing and user-friendly interface to improve the overall user experience.

Diversify your material to cater to various learning preferences. Incorporate engaging visuals, such as images and infographics, and consider making video material. Video marketing has become increasingly popular, and sites like YouTube provide additional avenues to reach and connect with your audience.

Optimise your website for search engines (SEO) to improve its visibility in search results. Research relevant keywords and incorporate them naturally into your writing. This will bring organic traffic to your website, increasing the possible reach of your affiliate promotions.

Implement a robust email marketing plan to build and nurture a subscriber list. Offer incentives, such as exclusive material or discounts, to urge visitors to subscribe. Regularly communicate with your email list, offering valuable material and occasional affiliate promotions.

3. Social Media Channels:

Social media sites offer an immediate and interactive way to connect with your audience. Popular sites include Instagram, Facebook, Twitter, Pinterest, and LinkedIn. Choosing the right platform relies on your niche and the preferences of your target audience.

Create dedicated social media accounts that reflect your brand and niche. Optimise your profiles with interesting visuals, a concise bio, and links to your blog or website. Consistent branding across platforms improves recognition and reinforces your online presence.

Craft a content plan tailored to each platform's strengths. Visual platforms like Instagram and Pinterest are ideal for showcasing product images and lifestyle content, while Twitter and Facebook allow real-time updates and interactions. Tailor your content to connect with the specific demographics and behaviours of each platform's user base.

Leverage social media scheduling tools to keep a consistent posting plan. Consistency is key to building and keeping an engaged social media following. Interact with your audience through comments, direct messages, and polls to create a sense of community.

Integrate affiliate links carefully within your social media posts. Craft captions that provide context and value, guiding your audience toward the promoted goods or services. Experiment with different types of content, such as tutorials, reviews, and user feedback, to diversify your promotional approach. Whichever platform you choose, it's important to prioritise quality over quantity. Consistent, valuable, and authentic material resonates with your audience and builds your credibility within your niche. As you build your platform, consider the following key principles:

1. Authenticity:

- Authenticity is the linchpin of good affiliate marketing.

Your audience is more likely to trust and engage with material that feels genuine. Share personal thoughts, experiences, and opinions to humanise your brand and connect with your audience on a deeper level.

2.   Value-Centric Approach:

- Prioritise providing value to your audience in every piece of content you make. Whether it's through educational articles, entertaining videos, or inspirational social media posts, the value you offer builds trust and places you as a valuable resource in your niche.

3. Consistency:

- Consistency is the key to building a recognizable brand and sustaining audience involvement. Maintain a consistent posting schedule, adhere to a cohesive visual design, anld ensure that your message aligns with your overall brand narrative.

4. Audience Engagement:

- Actively engage with your fans across your chosen platform. Respond to comments, join in discussions, and seek feedback. This interaction not only creates a sense of community but also provides valuable insights into your audience's preferences and needs.

5. Strategic Promotion:

- When incorporating affiliate links, take a strategic and thoughtful method. Integrate these links naturally within your content, ensuring that they improve the user experience rather than disrupt it. Craft compelling calls-to-action that encourage your audience to explore the suggested products or services.

As you build your platform, remember that affiliate marketing is a journey that changes over time. Continuously refine your strategies based on data, comments, and industry trends. Stay adaptable and open to experimentation, and let your platform be a dynamic mirror of your growth as an affiliate marketer.

In conclusion, building a platform is the bedrock of your affiliate marketing business. Whether through a blog, website, or social media channels, this platform becomes the canvas on which you share valuable content, connect with your audience, and carefully incorporate affiliate links. Choose the platform that fits with your goals and audience preferences, and infuse it with authenticity, value, and consistency. Your platform is not just a promotional place but a dynamic ecosystem where your affiliate marketing journey unfolds. So, start on this journey with purpose, passion, and a commitment to building a platform that resonates with your audience and stands the test of digital evolution.

Chapter 5:Create Quality Content

Making good content is a plan for involving

people in a way that adds value. Indeed though chapter marketing is always changing, the saying" content is king" still rings true. Your advertising sweats will only be successful if you can write content that not only gets people's attention but also gives them real value. This detailed companion goes into great depth about how to make good content, stressing how important it's to be applicable, real, and authentically interested in meeting your followership's requirements. 1. Knowing the

significance of Good Content-
further Than Just Marketing

Quality material goes beyond the normal ways of marketing. It's further than just a way to sell goods or services; it's also a way to make connections, earn trust, and place yourself as an expert in your field. The point is not just to make a trade; you want to ameliorate your followership's lives. —

Value as a Diffuser

People are constantly being swamped with information online, so the worth you give through your content is what sets you piecemeal. High- quality material sets you piecemeal, landing the attention of your followership and encouraging a sense of fidelity. It's the foundation upon which lasting connections with your observers are made.

- Long- Term Impact

The impact of quality material goes beyond immediate transformations. It contributes to business character, followership retention, and organic growth. When your followership sees your content as useful and dependable, they're more likely to return for unborn perceptivity, recommendations, and engagement.

2. Understanding Your followership - followership Persona Development

Before making content, claw into the complications of your followership's demographics, tastes, and pain points. Develop detailed followership personas that reflect the different groups within your target followership. Understanding your followership's wants and pretensions serves as the compass guiding your content creation path.

- **Empathy and Connection**

Cultivate empathy for your followership's obstacles and pretensions. The capability to empathise helps you to conform your content to address their pain points and offer answers. erecting a genuine relationship through compassionate content promotes trust, situating you as a dependable source within your niche.

- **Feedback and Engagement**

laboriously seek commentary and engage with your observers. Examiner commentary on your content, encourage exchanges, and pay attention to the questions or enterprises made by your followership. This two-way communication not only enhances the applicability of your content but also gives precious perceptivity for unborn creations.

3. Types of Quality Content - instructional papers and Attendants

Craft in- depth papers and attendants that give useful information within your area. Whether it's how- to tips, tutorials, or instructional pieces, these papers place you as an authority and resource for your followership.

- Product Reviews and Recommendations

Offer real and thorough product reviews. Your followership values authentic perceptivity into the goods or services you push. Transparent reviews make trust and help your followership in making informed choices.

- Engaging videos and Tutorials influence the power of videotape material. produce engaging and instructional flicks, whether they're product demonstrations, tutorials, or tutoring material. Visual content has a unique capability to allure cult and deliver information successfully.

-Curated Lists and Recommendations collect curated lists of recommended goods, services, or tools. These lists streamline decision- making for your followership, showing them with a curated collection that aligns with their requirements.

- Case Studies and Success Stories Share case studies and success stories. Real- life exemplifications add a mortal touch to your content, illustrating how goods or services have appreciatively affected others. Case studies make relatable narratives that connect with your followership.

- **Interactive Content**
Explore interactive content types similar as quizzes, pates, or checks. Interactive material not only engages your followership but also gives precious perceptivity into their preferences and views.

4. Authenticity in Content Creation - particular Voice and Style
inoculate your work with a particular voice

and style. Authenticity stems from the unique way you express studies and interact with your followership. Your personality should shine through, making a link that goes beyond transactional relations.

- **Honesty and translucency**

Prioritise honesty and translucency in your work.However, easily reveal your chapter connections, If you are promoting chapter goods. Honest and transparent communication builds trust and reinforces your resoluteness to give unprejudiced information.

- **Learning from Experience**

Partake your own tests and assignments learned. Whether it's successes, challenges, or particular stories, these perceptivity add to the authenticity of your material. Cult value relatable narratives that reflect real- world guests .

5. Optimising for Readability and Availability

- Clear and Concise Language

Strive for clarity and conciseness in your work. Use wording that's fluently understood by your target group. Avoid gratuitous slang and value simplicity without compromising the depth of your material.

- Readable Formatting

Format your textbook for readability. Break down big blocks of textbook into shorter paragraphs, use heads, and add pellet points or numbered lists. Readable formatting improves the stoner experience and makes your material more digestible.

- Mobile-Friendly Design

ensures that your information is mobile-friendly. With an adding quantum of drugs penetrating information on mobile bias, responsive design is important. Test the readability and usability of your material across colourful bias to feed to a different followership.

6. Strategic Use of Visual rudiments

- Engaging Images and plates Integrate engaging images and plates into your work. Visual rudiments not only ameliorate the aesthetic appeal but also communicate information more effectively. Use high-quality images, infographics, and important plates to support your written information.

- witching Thumbnails for videos still, invest in engaging thumbnails, If you make videotape content. Thumbnails serve as the first point of contact for implicit observers. A visually charming and applicable summary entices druggies to click and discover your videotape material.

- Data Visualization: Visualise data to make it more understandable. If your content involves showing statistics or data, use charts, graphs, or visual representations to share information. Visualising info helps in comprehension and retention.

7. SEO Strategies for Content Optimization:

- Keyword Research: Conduct thorough keyword study to find relevant terms and phrases within your niche. Integrate these keywords easily into your writing to optimise it for search engines. Strategic use of keywords improves the discoverability of your material.

-Meta Tags and Descriptions: Optimise meta tags and titles for your work. Craft engaging meta titles and descriptions that not only include important keywords but also entice users to click. Well-optimised meta tags add to better search engine rankings.

- Quality Backlinks: Build quality backlinks to your work. Quality backlinks from reputable sources signal to search engines that your content is valuable and authoritative. Focus on making material that naturally draws backlinks through its quality and relevance.

8. Promoting User Engagement:

- Call-to-Action Elements:

Integrate clear and compelling call-to-action (CTA) elements within your work. Whether it's encouraging users to subscribe, share, or explore affiliate goods, carefully placed CTAs guide user interactions and enhance engagement.

- **Encouraging Comments and Feedback:**

Encourage comments and feedback from your readers. Actively respond to comments to build a sense of community. User-generated discussions add depth to your material and provide additional views.

- **Social Media Integration:**

Integrate social media aspects into your content plan. Share your information across important social media sites, leveraging their reach to extend your audience. Encourage social sharing and involvement to amplify the effect of your material.

9. Consistency in Content Delivery:

- Establishing a Content Calendar:

Maintain consistency in your content release by setting a content calendar. Plan and plan your content in advance, ensuring a steady flow of useful information for your audience.

Consistency builds confidence and trust.

- **Content Variety and Diversity:**

Diversify your content offers to cater to different tastes within your audience. Experiment with various formats, themes, and styles to keep your content approach fresh and engaging. Variety avoids monotony and encourages continued interest.

-**Monitoring Trends and Relevance:**

Stay abreast of business trends and changing interests within your niche. Regularly assess the relevance of your information in relation to current changes. Being attuned to trends allows you to create material that stays timely and resonant with your audience.

10. Measuring and Analysing Performance:

- Utilising Analytics Tools:

Leverage analytics tools to measure the success of your material. Track key facts such as page hits, engagement rates, and conversion rates. Analytics provide insights into what connects with your audience and leads future content strategies.

- A/B Testing for Optimization:

Implement A/B testing to optimize your content methods. Experiment with changes in headlines, material structures, or promotional methods. A/B testing helps you to find high-performing elements and refine your approach for maximum effect.

-Feedback and Iterative Improvement:

Act on feedback and ideas gathered from success metrics. Embrace an iterative way to content improvement. Continuously refine your content strategies based on user comments, analytics, and new trends.

11. Adapting to Evolving Trends:

- Dynamic Nature of Content Trends:

Acknowledge the changing nature of material trends. Stay agile and adaptable to shifts in user tastes, platform algorithms, and content consumption habits. Adapting to evolving trends places you as a forward-thinking content author.

- Emerging Content Formats:

Explore emerging content forms and channels. As new

technologies and platforms appear, measure their relevance to your niche and audience. Embracing innovative content forms keeps your approach dynamic and fits with changing consumption habits.

-Balancing Evergreen and Trending Content: Strike a balance between evergreen and trending information. While evergreen content provides enduring value, adding trending themes allows you to stay relevant and capitalise on current interests. This balance ensures a well-rounded content strategy.

12. Conclusion:

- Elevating Your Affiliate Marketing Journey:

Creating quality content is not just a facet of affiliate marketing; it is the cornerstone of a successful and lasting affiliate journey. By knowing your audience, infusing authenticity into your content, and optimi6zing for readability and engagement, you raise your affiliate marketing efforts to new heights.

- Value as the Catalyst for Success:

The real catalyst for success in affiliate marketing lies in the value you give to your audience through your content. As you manage the intricacies of content creation, remember that each piece adds to a mosaic of engagement, trust, and lasting connections with your audience.

- **Empowering Your Audience and Yourself:**

Ultimately, the power of quality material lies in its ability to empower both your viewers and yourself. As you share important insights, suggestions, and experiences, you become a guiding force within your niche. In this reciprocal relationship, your audience gets knowledge and solutions, while you forge a path of credibility, effect, and sustained success in the dynamic world of affiliate marketing.

Chapter 6: Use SEO Strategies

Leveraging SEO (Search Engine Optimization) strategies is an integral component of a good affiliate marketing approach. In a vast digital landscape where visibility is key, optimizing your material for search engines becomes a strategic imperative. By employing relevant keywords, crafting compelling meta tags, and cultivating high-quality backlinks, you can enhance your site's visibility and attract organic traffic, setting the groundwork for sustained success in the competitive world of online marketing.

1. Keyword Research:
- Foundation of SEO:
Keyword research forms the bedrock of successful SEO. By identifying and strategically incorporating relevant keywords within your content, you increase the likelihood of your

platform being found by users looking for information in your niche.

- Understanding User Intent:
Dive into the minds of your target group and understand their intent. What are they searching for, and how can your content provide useful answers? Align your chosen keywords with the questions and needs of your audience to create material that fulfills their expectations.

- Long-Tail Keywords:
Don't dismiss the power of long-tail keywords. While short and generic keywords may have

higher search volumes, long-tail keywords are often more specific and reflect user intent more correctly. Integrating a mix of both types of keywords gives a well-rounded SEO strategy.

- Competitor Analysis: Analyse the keywords your rivals are targeting. Tools like SEMrush, Ahrefs, or Google Keyword Planner can provide insights into the keywords that are driving traffic to rival platforms. This analysis informs your keyword approach and helps find opportunities for differentiation.

2. On-Page Optimization:

- Strategic Placement:
Once you've discovered your goal keywords, strategically incorporate them into your content. Place keywords in titles, headings, meta descriptions, and naturally within the body of your writing. This strategic placement signals to search engines that your content is important to users' queries.

- User-Friendly URLs:
Craft user-friendly URLs that include important keywords. Clear and concise URLs not only add to a positive user experience but also enhance the overall SEO of your

content. Avoid lengthy, complex URLs that may confuse both users and search engines.

- Optimised Images:
Optimise pictures by using descriptive file names and adding alt text. Search engines also consider image optimization when ranking material. Descriptive file names and alt text provide additional context, adding to the overall relevance of your page.

- Internal Linking:
Integrate internal links carefully within your content. Link to other related articles or pages on your platform. Internal linking not only

improves the user experience by guiding visitors to related content but also distributes SEO value throughout your site.

- Mobile Optimization: Ensure that your platform is mobile-friendly. With a growing number of users viewing content via mobile devices, mobile optimization is a crucial factor in search engine rankings. Responsive design and mobile-friendly layouts add to a positive user experience across various devices.

3. Quality Content Creation:

- Content is King:

Quality content is not just a catchphrase—it's a basic truth in the world of SEO. Search engines favour content that is informative, engaging, and valuable to users. Craft content that addresses user queries, offers solutions, and aligns with the purpose behind search queries.

- **Diverse Content Formats:**

Diversify your content formats to cater to different user tastes. In addition to written pieces, consider incorporating visuals, such as infographics, videos, and podcasts. Varied content formats add to a richer user experience and can attract a broader audience.

- User Engagement: Encourage user engagement with your material. High amounts of engagement, such as longer time spent on your site, low bounce rates, and social media shares, are positive signals to search engines. Create content that captivates your viewers and encourages them to explore more.

- Evergreen Content: Include evergreen material in your strategy. Evergreen content stays relevant over time and continues to attract organic traffic.

Foundational guides, comprehensive overviews, and informative articles add to a sustainable SEO strategy.

4. Meta Tags and Descriptions:

- Compelling Titles:
Craft compelling titles that not only include important keywords but also entice users to click through. Your title is often the first thing users see in search results, making it a critical element in catching their attention.

- Meta Descriptions:
Write concise and engaging meta descriptions. While meta descriptions may

not directly impact search engine rankings, they serve as a snippet that users read before choosing whether to click through. A well-crafted meta description can greatly improve click-through rates.

- Local SEO:

If your affiliate marketing efforts have a local focus, improve your content for local SEO. Include location-specific keywords, make a Google My Business profile, and encourage positive reviews. Local SEO tactics improve your visibility in location-based searches.

5. Backlink Building:

- Importance of Backlinks:

Backlinks, or inbound links, from reputable and authoritative websites are a strong signal to search engines. They suggest that your work is valued and trusted within your niche. Building a portfolio of high-quality backlinks is an ongoing process that adds to the credibility of your platform.

- Natural Link-Building:

Focus on natural link-building tactics. Creating quality content naturally attracts backlinks as other websites reference and link to your valuable resources. Outreach, collaborations, and guest posting are additional strategies to promote backlink possibilities.

- **Quality Over Quantity:**
Prioritize the quality of backlinks over sheer number. A few high-quality, relevant backlinks from authoritative sites carry more weight than numerous low-quality links. Focus on building relationships within your niche to cultivate meaningful backlink possibilities.

- **Monitor and Disavow:**

Regularly watch your backlink profile using tools like Google Search Console. If you discover low-quality or spammy backlinks, consider disavowing them. Maintaining a clean backlink profile adds to a good SEO reputation.

6. Technical SEO:

- Site Speed:

Optimize your site's speed for a good user experience. Search engines view page load times as a ranking factor. Compress images, leverage browser caching, and utilize content delivery networks (CDNs) to improve your site's speed.

- Sitemap:

Submit a link to search engines. A sitemap gives a structured overview of your site's content, making it easier for search engines to crawl and index your pages. Submitting a sitemap through Google Search Console helps in the discoverability of your content.

- SSL Encryption:

Secure your site with SSL security. In addition to offering a secure browsing experience for users, SSL encryption is a factor considered by search engines. Websites with SSL certificates may receive a slight boost in search results.

- Structured Data:
Implement structured data markup to improve the visibility of your material in search engine results. Structured data provides additional context to search engines, allowing them to present richer snippets, such as star ratings, publication dates, and featured snippets.

7. Analytics and Continuous Improvement:

- Data-Driven Insights:
Leverage analytics tools to gather data-driven insights into your platform's success.

Tools like Google Analytics provide useful information on user behavior, traffic sources, and engagement metrics. Analyzing this data guides your SEO strategy and content optimization efforts.

- A/B Testing:
Experiment with A/B testing to refine your SEO tactics. Test variations of titles, meta descriptions, and content structures to identify what connects most with your audience. A/B testing helps you to make informed decisions based on user

preferences and engagement.

- Adaptability:

Stay adaptable to algorithm updates and business trends. The field of SEO is dynamic, and search engine algorithms change. Staying informed about changes and adapting your strategy accordingly ensures that your platform stays optimized for current best practices.

In conclusion, using SEO strategies is not a one-time job but an ongoing commitment to optimizing your platform for visibility and relevance. By incorporating relevant keywords, creating compelling meta tags, cultivating high-quality backlinks, and continuously refining your approach based on analytics and industry trends, you place your affiliate marketing platform for long-term success. SEO is not just a technical aspect of digital marketing; it's a dynamic and strategic endeavour that aligns your content with the needs and demands of your audience while ensuring your platform stands out in the competitive online landscape.

Chapter 7: Promote Affiliate Products

Effectively promoting affiliate goods requires a delicate balance between seamless integration and transparent communication with your audience. As an affiliate marketer, your goal is not only to create revenue through affiliate links but also to provide value to your audience. By integrating affiliate links naturally within your content and keeping transparency about your affiliate relationships, you can foster trust, build credibility, and create a mutually beneficial relationship with your audience.

1. Seamless Integration:

- Contextual Relevance:

Integrate affiliate links in a way that fits with the overall context of your content. Whether you're writing a product review, a tutorial, or an informative article, the addition of affiliate links should feel natural and enhance the user experience rather than disrupt it.

- Strategic Placement:

Consider the smart placement of affiliate links within your

content. Position them where they provide the most value to your viewers. For example, in a product review, include affiliate links at the appropriate places where readers are likely to explore further or make a purchase decision.

- **Anchor Text Optimization:**
Optimise anchor text to make it useful and compelling. Instead of generic terms like "click here" or "check it out," use descriptive anchor text that explains the nature of the linked content. This not only improves user experience but also adds

to the SEO value of your links.

- Visual Elements:
Enhance the integration of affiliate links with visual features. If you're promoting physical goods, include images or videos that showcase the things. Visuals not only capture attention but also provide extra context, making the affiliate link integration more engaging.

- Variety in Content Formats:
Diversify the formats of your material to accommodate different preferences. Whether it's written articles, videos, podcasts, or infographics, adapt your

affiliate link integration to fit the medium. Each format presents unique possibilities for seamless integration.

2. Transparency and Authenticity:

- Clear Disclosure: Prioritise transparency with your viewers about your affiliate relationships. Clearly disclose the presence of affiliate links within your work. This can be done through a brief disclaimer at the beginning of your piece or a note near the affiliate links.

-Honest Reviews and Recommendations: Maintain honesty and authenticity in your reviews and suggestions. Share your genuine experiences and opinions about the goods or services you're promoting. Authenticity builds trust with your audience and ensures that your suggestions are credible.

- Affiliate Relationship Disclaimer:

Include a brief disclaimer explaining your affiliate connections. This could say that you may earn a commission if users make a purchase through your affiliate links. Such disclaimers are not only ethical but also required by regulatory authorities in many areas.

- **Avoid Overpromotion**:
Be mindful of the regularity and density of affiliate links in your content. Avoid overloading your audience with promotions, as this may lessen the trust you've built. Prioritise offering useful content, and let affiliate promotions complement rather than dominate your platform.

- **Personal Touch:**
Infuse a human touch into your affiliate promotions. Share personal anecdotes or stories related to the goods you're endorsing.

This not only humanises your material but also strengthens the connection between you and your audience.

3. Educate and Inform
-   Value-Driven Content:
Prioritise creating value-driven content that educates and informs your community. When promoting affiliate goods, focus on how they address particular needs or solve problems. Emphasise the value that users will gain from exploring the recommended goods or services.

-   In-Depth Information:

Provide in-depth information about the affiliate goods. Instead of merely listing features, delve into how these features help the user. Whether through detailed specifications, use cases, or real-world examples, offer thorough insights to guide your audience's decision-making.

- User Benefits:

Clearly articulate the benefits that users can expect from the affiliate goods. Whether it's saving time, improving efficiency, or enhancing a particular area of their lives, emphasise how the products align with the needs and desires of your target audience.

- **Comparisons and Alternatives:** Include product comparisons or alternatives in your material. This demonstrates that you've thoroughly studied and considered various options, further guiding your audience in their decision-making process. Such comparisons add depth to your suggestions.

4. Build Trust Through Consistency:

- Consistent Branding: Maintain consistent branding across your site. This includes the visual presentation of your material, your tone of voice, and the overall messaging. Consistency builds brand recognition and reinforces the trust your audience places in your advice.

- Reliable Information: Build a reputation for giving reliable information. Consistency in providing accurate and helpful content enhances your credibility. Trust is a valuable tool in affiliate marketing, and consistent reliability strengthens the foundation of that trust.

- Responsive Communication:

Be responsive to audience inquiries and comments. Engage with your followers through comments, social media, or email. Addressing questions or concerns shows your commitment to providing value and fosters a sense of community.

- **Affiliate Product Updates:**

Stay informed about updates or changes linked to the affiliate products you promote. If there are new features, improvements, or related news, share this information with your audience. Keeping them in the loop reinforces your dedication to giving up-to-date and accurate recommendations.

5. Strategic Call-to-Action (CTA):

- Guided Action:

Craft strategic calls-to-action that guide your viewers toward the desired action. Whether it's exploring affiliate links, making a purchase, or subscribing to a newsletter, your CTAs should be clear, compelling, and aligned with the general user journey.

- Incentives for Action:

Provide rewards for taking action through your affiliate links. This could include exclusive discounts, special offers, or access to premium material. Incentives not only encourage engagement but also enhance the perceived value of the recommended goods.

- Variety of CTAs: Diversify the types of CTAs you use. Experiment with different wording, formats, and placements to identify what connects best with your audience. A variety of CTAs ensures that you cater to different user behaviours and tastes.

- Educational CTAs: Incorporate teaching CTAs that explain the benefits of using your affiliate links. Help your audience understand how these links support your platform and allow you to continue providing valuable content. Education creates transparency and empowers your audience to make informed choices.

6.Monitor Performance and Adapt:

- Analytics Insights: Utilise analytics tools to watch the success of your affiliate promotions. Track metrics such as click-through rates, conversion rates, and revenue produced through affiliate links. Analysing this data provides insights into the success of your strategies.

- A/B Testing:

Experiment with A/B testing to refine your promotional tactics. Test variations of titles, content structures, or CTAs to identify what connects most with your audience. A/B testing helps you to make data-driven decisions and continuously optimise your approach.

- Adapt to Audience Feedback:

Pay attention to audience comments and adapt accordingly. If your audience expresses preferences or concerns related to your affiliate promotions, use this feedback to improve your strategies. An adaptive approach shows your commitment to meeting the needs of your readers.

- Stay Informed About Products:
Stay informed about updates, new releases, or changes linked to the affiliate items you promote. Being knowledgeable about the products guarantees that your content stays accurate and relevant. It also positions you as a reliable source of knowledge within your niche.

In conclusion, promoting affiliate

goods successfully involves a careful blend of seamless integration, transparency, and a commitment to giving value. By seamlessly incorporating affiliate links within your content, keeping transparency about your affiliate relationships, and prioritizing value-driven content, you can build a trusting relationship with your audience. Remember, the essence of successful affiliate marketing lies not just in generating revenue but in creating a symbiotic relationship where both you and your audience profit.

Chapter 8:
Build an Email List

Building an email list is a powerful strategy for affiliate marketers looking to create a direct and personalized connection with their audience. An email list serves as a dedicated channel to share valuable content, build relationships, and occasionally promote affiliate goods. By collecting email addresses from interested visitors and nurturing your email list strategically, you can build a loyal community that engages with your content and responds positively to affiliate promotions.

1. The Significance of an Email List:

-   Direct Communication:

An email list offers a direct and personal communication channel with your audience. Unlike social media platforms or search engines, where algorithms decide reach, emails land directly in your subscribers' inboxes. This direct line of communication allows for a more intimate relationship with your audience.

-   Ownership and Control:

Unlike social media fans or website traffic, your email list is an asset you own and control. Platforms may change their algorithms, policies, or even cease to exist, but your email list stays a stable and dependable asset. This ownership gives a sense of security and continuity.

- **Relationship Building:**

Building an email list allows you to build relationships with your audience over time. Regularly delivering valuable material establishes trust and credibility. This relationship-building aspect is crucial when it comes to introducing affiliate goods, as your audience is more likely to engage with recommendations from a trusted source.

-          **Targeted Communication:** With email segmentation and personalization tools, you can tailor your messages to specific segments of your community. This targeted method ensures that your subscribers receive material and promotions that align with their interests and preferences, enhancing the relevance of your communications.

2. Collecting Email Addresses:

- Opt-In Forms:

Strategically place opt-in forms on your website to encourage visitors to join. These forms can be inserted within blog posts, in the sidebar, or as pop-ups. Clearly explain the value of subscribing, whether it's access to exclusive content, updates, or special offers.

- Lead Magnets:

Offer lead magnets as rewards for subscription. This could include downloadable guides, ebooks, checklists, or exclusive material. Lead magnets entice visitors to provide their email addresses in exchange for valuable resources, instantly adding them to your email list.

- **Contests and Giveaways:**

Run contests or giveaways that require users to enter with their email addresses. This not only expands your email list but also generates excitement and engagement within your community. Ensure that the prizes are related to your niche to attract truly interested subscribers.

- **Webinars and Events:**

Host webinars, internet events, or workshops and use the registration process to collect email addresses. Events provide an opportunity to showcase your expertise, and the registration process helps grow your email list with individuals interested in your field.

- **Social Media Integration:** Integrate email sign-up opportunities across your social media platforms. Use platforms like Instagram, Facebook, or Twitter to push your lead magnets or direct followers to subscribe to your newsletter for exclusive updates and content.

3. Nurturing Your Email List:

- Welcome Series:
Implement a welcome series for new members. Introduce yourself, set expectations for the type of content they'll receive, and deliver instant value. This series helps in creating a positive first impression and engages new subscribers from the outset.

- Valuable Content:
Consistently provide valuable material to your email subscribers. Whether it's exclusive articles, tips, or insights, make sure your emails

offer something important. This regular delivery of value keeps your audience engaged and reinforces the trust they've put in your content.

- Segmentation:

Use segmentation to tailor your emails based on subscriber tastes and behaviours. Segmenting your list allows you to send targeted content and promotions to particular groups, increasing the relevance of your communications. Segmentation could be based on hobbies, engagement level, or other factors.

- Personalization:

Personalize your texts whenever possible. Address subscribers by their names and customize content based on their past interactions. Personalization produces a more individualized experience, making your audience feel valued and understood.

- Consistent Schedule: Establish a consistent email schedule to keep engagement. Whether you choose to send texts weekly, bi-weekly, or monthly, consistency is key. Subscribers become accustomed to your contact rhythm, and a predictable plan helps in managing expectations.

4. Occasional Affiliate Promotions:

- Strategic Timing: Introduce affiliate promotions carefully within your email campaigns. Avoid bombarding your users with constant promotions, as this may lead to disengagement. Instead, time your affiliate promotions carefully, aligning them with relevant content or special offers.

- Educational Approach: Take an educational method when promoting affiliate products. Instead of simply showing the product, provide context on how it addresses a particular need or solves a problem. Share your personal experiences or thoughts to make the promotion more relatable and trustworthy.

- Exclusive Offers: Provide exclusive offers or deals for your email subscribers. This adds value to your email communications and incentivizes subscribers to connect with your affiliate promotions. Exclusive offers build a sense of privilege for your email audience.

- Affiliate Product Reviews:

Incorporate partner product reviews into your email content. Share in-depth insights, pros and cons, and your personal experiences with the goods you're promoting. Genuine reviews add to the authenticity of your recommendations and build trust with your audience.

- **Limited-Time Campaigns:**

Introduce limited-time campaigns or promotions for affiliate goods. Creating a sense of urgency pushes subscribers to take action promptly. Include clear calls-to-action and deadlines to convey the time-sensitive nature of the offer.

5. Maintaining Compliance:

- Legal Requirements: Familiarize yourself with legal requirements linked to email marketing, such as anti-spam laws. Ensure that your email campaigns comply with regulations to avoid possible legal problems. Include an unsubscribe option in every email and honor opt-out requests quickly.

- Permission-Based Marketing: Practice permission-based marketing by only sending emails to people who have explicitly opted in to receive them.

Building your email list with permission ensures that your subscribers are truly interested in your content, increasing the chance of positive engagement.

- **Privacy and Data Security:**
Prioritize the privacy and data protection of your subscribers. Clearly explain your privacy policy, detailing how you handle subscriber information. Implement security measures to protect the data saved within your email marketing platform.

- **Consent for Promotions:**

Explicitly seek consent for getting promotional emails, including affiliate promotions. Not all subscribers may be interested in promotional material, and respecting their preferences adds to a positive subscriber experience.

6. Analytics and Optimization:

- Email Analytics:
Utilize email analytics tools to track the success of your campaigns. Monitor measures such as open rates, click-through rates, and conversion rates. Analyzing these metrics provides insights into the success

of your email marketing strategies.

- A/B Testing:
Experiment with A/B testing to optimize your email marketing. Test variations in subject lines, content, or calls-to-action to identify what connects best with your audience. A/B testing helps you to refine your approach based on data-driven insights.

- Subscriber Feedback:
Encourage and receive feedback from your subscribers. Use surveys or direct contact to understand their preferences, expectations, and

comments regarding your email content. Subscriber feedback is essential for making informed adjustments to your email strategy.

- **Adaptation to Trends:**
Stay updated about email marketing trends and best practices. The field evolves, and staying adaptive ensures that your email marketing strategy stays effective in a dynamic digital landscape. Be open to incorporating new tools and methods that enhance your email campaigns.

In conclusion, building an email list is a dynamic process that includes strategic collection, consistent nurturing, and occasional affiliate promotions. By prioritising direct communication, providing valuable material, and respecting legal and ethical considerations, you can build an engaged and responsive email community. Remember, an email list is not just a means of promotion; it's a relationship-building tool that allows you to connect with your audience on a deeper level, encouraging loyalty and trust over time.

Chapter 9:Engage on Social Media

Leveraging social media platforms is a pivotal strategy for affiliate marketers wanting to extend their reach and cultivate a loyal following. In the dynamic landscape of digital marketing, social media serves as a powerful tool to connect with audiences, share valuable content, and build a brand presence. By strategically sharing content and actively engaging with your audience on platforms like Instagram, Facebook, Twitter, and others, you can not only enhance your visibility but also build a community that trusts and values your ideas.

1. Choose the Right Platforms:

- Understand Your Audience:
Identify the social media sites most frequented by your target group. Understanding the demographics, tastes, and behaviors of your community helps you choose the platforms where your efforts will yield the highest effect. Different platforms cater to distinct user groups and content consumption habits.

- Niche Relevance:

Consider the importance of your niche on different platforms. Some niches thrive on visual material, making platforms like Instagram and Pinterest ideal, while others may benefit more from the text-focused environment of Twitter or the professional networking possibilities on LinkedIn.

- **Platform-Specific Features:** Familiarise yourself with the features and functions of each site. Instagram, for instance, emphasises visuals and storytelling through photos and short videos, while Twitter is known for concise, real-time messages. Tailor your content to leverage the unique traits of each site.

- Consistent Branding: Maintain consistent branding across all social media platforms. Use consistent profile pictures, cover photos, and bio information. Consistency builds recognition, reinforcing your brand identity and making it easier for followers to know and engage with your content.

2. Share Valuable Content:

- Diversify Content Formats:

Diversify your content forms to cater to different tastes. Share a mix of text-based posts, pictures, videos, infographics, and interactive stuff. Varied content formats keep your feed engaging and appeal to a larger audience with different consumption habits.

- Educational Content: Provide educational material that aligns with the interests and wants of your audience. Whether it's tips, tutorials, or industry views, positioning yourself as an informative resource promotes trust and encourages your audience to turn to you for valuable information.

- Visual Appeal:
Prioritise visual attraction in your work. High-quality images, aesthetically pleasing designs, and compelling visuals catch attention in the fast-scrolling atmosphere of social media. Invest time in creating or curating visuals that connect with your business and audience.

- Consistent Posting Schedule:
Establish a regular posting plan. Regularity in your posting cadence keeps your audience engaged and

accustomed to seeing your content. Consistency is key in building a social media presence that stays relevant in the thoughts of your followers.

3. Engage Authentically:

- Respond to Comments: Actively reply to comments on your posts. Engage with your audience by answering questions, showing gratitude for positive comments, and fostering discussions. Responding to comments shows that you value and respect the interactions with your followers.

- Ask Questions:

Encourage audience interaction by asking questions. Pose thoughtful and relevant questions in your captions or comments to start discussions. Engaging your audience in conversations not only builds community but also provides useful insights into their preferences and views.

- Host Q&A Sessions: Host Q&A sessions to directly answer your audience's questions. This interactive format allows you to connect with your fans on a more personal way. Consider using features like Instagram Stories' question sticker or

Twitter polls to help Q&A sessions.

- **User-Generated Content:**
Encourage user-generated content by inviting your followers to share their stories or use your goods. Reposting user-generated content not only shows the authenticity of your brand but also strengthens the sense of community among your fans.

4. Strategic Use of Hashtags:

- **Research Relevant Hashtags:**
Research and use important hashtags in your posts. Hashtags

improve the discoverability of your content by categorising it within specific themes or trends. Identify famous hashtags within your niche and incorporate them carefully to broaden your reach.

- **Create Branded Hashtags:**
Create customised hashtags specific to your partner marketing efforts. Branded hashtags not only foster community participation but also make it easier for followers to find content related to your promotions. Include your branded hashtags in posts related to

affiliate items or campaigns.

- Trending Hashtags:
Capitalise on popular hashtags when important to your content. Stay updated about current trends and events within your business or niche. Using trending hashtags can increase the visibility of your posts, exposing your content to a bigger audience.

- Hashtag Limits:
While hashtags can improve exposure, avoid excessive use. Each site has its own best practices regarding the number of hashtags to include. Experiment with different hashtag

quantities to find the optimal mix for your content.

5. Collaborate with Influencers and Brands:

- Partnerships and Collaborations: Collaborate with leaders or brands within your field. Partnering with influencers allows you to tap into their current audience, expanding your reach and reputation. Look for influencers whose ideals match with your brand to ensure authentic collaborations.

- Affiliate Campaigns: Launch partner ads in collaboration with brands. Develop relationships that go beyond one-time promotions, and instead, create long-term connections.

Collaborative affiliate efforts can include joint giveaways, co-created content, or exclusive offers for your combined fans.

- Guest Posts:

Offer to make guest posts or takeovers on other related accounts. This cross-promotional method exposes your content to a new audience, often leading to increased followers and engagement. Ensure that the accounts you work with share a similar target group for optimal results.

- Mutual Promotion:
Engage in mutual marketing with stars or brands. Share each other's content, tag one another in relevant posts, and actively join in each other's efforts. This reciprocal way promotes a feeling of community and strengthens collaborative relationships.

6. Host Contests and Giveaways:

- Increase Engagement:
Host contests or giveaways to improve connection and reach. Contests encourage

followers to interact actively by liking, sharing, or commenting on your posts. The increased interaction not only improves visibility but also draws new followers.

- Partner with Brands: Collaborate with affiliate brands to run events. This collaborative approach benefits both parties, as it uses the brand's audience and provides a chance for followers to connect with your content and participate in the contest.

- Clear Entry Requirements: Clearly explain entry rules for contests or giveaways. Whether it's following your account, tagging friends, or sharing the post, make the entry process easy. Clearly stated requirements streamline participation, resulting in a higher level of engagement.

- **Prizes and Incentives:**
Offer enticing prizes or bonuses for event winners. The prizes could include things from affiliate partners, exclusive discounts, or other useful offerings. Ensure that the prizes match with the hobbies and preferences of your audience for maximum effect.

7. Monitor Analytics and Adjust Strategies:

- Platform Analytics:

Leverage platform analytics to monitor the success of your material. Each social media site offers insights into metrics such as reach, involvement, and follower growth. Regularly study these analytics to spot trends and learn which types of content connect most with your audience.

- Content Performance:

Evaluate the success of your content, including posts related to affiliate goods. Analyze which posts cause higher engagement and click-through rates. This data informs your content strategy, allowing you to refine your approach and highlight material that resonates with your audience.

- **Optimize Posting Times:**

Experiment with posting times to discover when your audience is most busy. The optimal posting times may change based on your target audience's geographic area, industry, and online habits. Use analytics to refine your posting plan and maximize the exposure of your content.

- A/B Testing:

Implement A/B testing for different content methods. Test changes in captions, visuals, posting frequencies, or material themes to understand what works best. A/B testing helps you to fine-tune your social media strategy based on data-driven insights.

8. Educate and Inform:

- Share Informative Content:

Prioritize sharing material that educates and informs your community. Whether it's industry trends, product insights, or tips related to your niche, positioning yourself as a useful source of information adds to your credibility and authority.

- Affiliate Product Insights:

Provide in-depth views into affiliate goods. Instead of merely promoting goods, share specific information about their features, benefits, and real-world applications. Educating your audience helps them make informed choices and builds trust in your advice.

- Tutorials and How-Tos:

Create tutorials or how-to tips related to affiliate goods. Visual demonstrations or step-by-step guides add value to your material and improve the user experience. Educational material not only draws engagement but also places you as an expert within your niche.

- Industry News and Updates:

Stay abreast of business news and changes. Sharing relevant news keeps your audience informed about the latest developments in your area. This type of content establishes your social media accounts as reliable sources for current information.

In conclusion, engaging on social media includes a strategic combination of material sharing, public interaction, and collaboration efforts. By choosing the right platforms, consistently providing valuable material, truly engaging with your audience, and adapting your strategies based on analytics, you can build a strong and loyal following. Social media is not just a promotional tool; it's a dynamic space where you can build meaningful connections, create your brand, and foster a community that actively engages with your affiliate marketing efforts.

Chapter 10: Analyse and Optimise

Analysing and optimising your affiliate marketing strategies is a basic step in ensuring long-term success and effectiveness. By leveraging analytics tools, affiliate marketers can gain valuable insights into the performance of their campaigns, find areas for improvement, and refine their strategies to maximize effect. This process of continuous analysis and optimization is key to staying adaptive in the dynamic world of digital marketing.

1. Importance of Analytics in Affiliate Marketing:

- Data-Driven Decision Making:

Analytics tools provide the facts necessary for informed decision-making. Instead of relying on assumptions or intuition, affiliate marketers can use real-time data to understand how their campaigns are working, where their audience is most engaged, and which strategies are driving the desired outcomes.

- Performance Evaluation:

Analytics allow for a thorough evaluation of performance metrics.

From click-through rates and conversion rates to audience demographics and geographic locations, marketers can assess various key performance indicators (KPIs) to measure the success of their affiliate marketing efforts.

- Identifying Trends and Patterns:

Analyzing data over time helps in finding trends and patterns. Understanding the peaks and valleys in performance can show seasonal trends, specific content preferences, or the impact of external factors. Recognizing these patterns allows marketers to adjust their strategies accordingly.

- Budget Allocation:
Analytics play a crucial part in optimizing budget allocation. By finding high-performing channels or campaigns, marketers can allocate resources more efficiently. This ensures that budget is directed towards strategies that give the best results, maximizing the return on investment (ROI).

2. Choosing the Right Analytics Tools:

- Google Analytics:
Google Analytics is a strong and widely used analytics tool. It offers comprehensive insights into website traffic, user

behavior, and conversion tracking. Marketers can watch the performance of affiliate links, monitor user engagement, and gain a holistic view of their online presence.

- **Affiliate Network Analytics:**
Many affiliate programs and networks offer their own tracking tools. These platforms provide specific insights into the success of affiliate links, conversion rates, and earnings. Marketers should leverage the analytics tools offered by their affiliate networks for detailed campaign tracking.

- Social Media Analytics:

Social media sites, such as Facebook Insights, Twitter Analytics, and Instagram Insights, offer analytics features. These tools provide statistics on post engagement, audience demographics, and the success of promoted content. Marketers can use social media analytics to refine their content plan.

- Email Marketing Analytics:

Email marketing platforms, including Mailchimp, Constant Contact, and others, provide analytics on email efforts. Marketers can track open rates, click-through rates, and conversion data. Analyzing email marketing data helps in improving email content and targeting.

3. Key Metrics to Track:

- Click-Through Rate (CTR):

CTR measures the percentage of users who click on a particular link compared to the total number of users who view a page, email, or advertisement.

Monitoring CTR offers insights into the effectiveness of calls-to-action and the appeal of affiliate links to your audience.

- Conversion Rate:

Conversion rate is the percentage of visitors who take a wanted action, such as making a purchase or filling out a form. Tracking conversion rates helps in understanding the success of your affiliate ads in driving the intended outcomes.

- **Revenue and Earnings:**
Tracking revenue and earnings generated through affiliate marketing is important. This metric gives a clear understanding of the financial impact of your campaigns. It helps in evaluating the profitability of different

affiliate partnerships and tactics.

- Audience Demographics:
Understanding the demographics of your community is important for targeted marketing. Analytics tools can provide insights into the age, gender, location, and interests of your community. This information guides content creation and customization to better resonate with your target group.

- Bounce Rate:
Bounce rate measures the percentage of visitors who navigate away from the site after watching only one page.

A high bounce rate may indicate that visitors are not getting what they expected. Analyzing bounce rates helps in optimizing landing pages and better user experience.

4. Continuous Monitoring and Reporting:

- Regular Reports:
Set up regular reporting schedules to watch key metrics consistently. Whether it's weekly, monthly, or quarterly, having a routine for reviewing performance data allows for timely identification of trends and the prompt application of optimization strategies.

- Custom Dashboards:
Create custom dashboards within analytics tools to consolidate relevant data in one view. Custom dashboards save time and provide a snapshot of the most important performance indicators. Marketers can adjust dashboards to focus on specific goals or areas of interest.

- Automated Alerts:
Utilize automated alerts to receive notices when specific metrics deviate from expected values. Automated alerts allow marketers to react promptly to significant changes in performance, addressing issues or

capitalizing on opportunities in real-time.

5. Identifying What Works:

- Top-Performing Channels: Analyze which marketing channels are giving the best results. Whether it's organic search, social media, email, or other channels, finding top-performing sources allows marketers to allocate resources more effectively.

- High-Performing Content: Determine which types of content resonate most with your readers. Identify high-performing blog posts, videos, or social media material. Analyzing content success helps in tailoring future content tactics to align with audience preferences.

- **Effective Affiliate Partnerships:** Evaluate the success of affiliate partnerships. Identify which affiliates regularly drive traffic, conversions, and revenue. Focusing on effective partnerships allows marketers to nurture relationships with high-performing affiliates and explore possibilities for collaboration.

- **Optimal Campaign Timing:**

Analyse the timing of ads and promotions. Identify whether certain times of the day, week, or year give better results. Understanding optimal timing helps marketers to plan campaigns when their audience is most receptive.

6. Areas for Improvement:

- Underperforming Content:

Identify content that is not performing as planned. Analyze the reasons behind underperformance, whether it's low engagement, high bounce rates, or other things. Adjust content strategies based on findings to improve performance.

- Low Conversion Points:

Analyse the turning points in your funnel. If certain stages of the customer journey have lower conversion rates, investigate possible obstacles or places for improvement.

Optimizing conversion points can have a major effect on overall campaign success.

- High Bounce Rates:

Address high bounce rates by reviewing landing page design, content relevance, and user experience. A high bounce rate may indicate that visitors are not finding what they expected or facing barriers to engagement.

- Ineffective Keywords:

For those utilizing SEO strategies, analyze the success of keywords. Identify keywords that are not driving major traffic or conversions. Adjust content and SEO strategies to focus on keywords that align with audience purpose and interests.

7. Optimization Strategies:

- Content Refinement:

Refine content based on performance data. Optimize headlines, imagery, and calls-to-action to align with what connects most with your audience. A/B testing different aspects can provide insights into the most effective content variations.

- **Landing Page Optimization:** Optimize landing pages to improve response rates. Ensure that landing pages are user-friendly, load fast, and provide a seamless experience. Experiment with different layouts, messaging, and visual features to discover the most effective configurations.

- **Adjusting Campaign Timing:**

Based on analysis, adjust the timing of your ads. Consider scheduling promotions during peak engagement times or aligning them with important industry events or holidays. Strategic timing can improve visibility and response rates.

- **Affiliate Partner Communication:** Communicate with affiliate partners based on success insights. Provide feedback, share successful strategies, and cooperate on ways to optimize campaigns. Building open communication with affiliates creates stronger relationships and mutual success.

8. Continuous Learning and Adaptation:

- Stay Informed About Industry Trends:

Stay informed about industry trends and changes in the digital marketing environment. Continuous learning ensures that your strategies remain relevant and effective in the face of changing consumer behaviors, search engine algorithms, and market dynamics.

- Experiment with New Strategies:

Embrace a spirit of experimentation. Test

new strategies, platforms, or content formats based on rising trends or industry innovations. Experimentation helps marketers to discover untapped opportunities and stay ahead of the curve.

- **Feedback and Collaboration:**
Encourage comments and collaboration within your team. Regular discussions about performance data, insights, and optimization strategies promote a collaborative atmosphere. Team members can offer diverse perspectives and ideas for improvement.

- Adaptation to External Factors:
Be adaptable in answer to external factors. Changes in consumer behavior, market trends, or regulatory landscapes can impact the performance of affiliate marketing efforts. A willingness to adapt ensures resilience in the face of unforeseen obstacles.

In conclusion, the cycle of analyzing and optimizing is a constant and integral aspect of successful affiliate marketing. By leveraging analytics tools, identifying what works, addressing areas for improvement, and implementing optimization strategies, marketers can refine their approaches, enhance performance, and stay agile in the ever-evolving digital environment. This commitment to data-driven decision-making guarantees that affiliate marketing efforts are not only effective but also positioned for sustained growth and success over time.

Chapter 11: Stay Updated

Staying streamlined in the changing field of chapter marketing is a foundation of success. The digital geography is continually evolving, with assiduity trends, new goods, and changes in chapter programs shaping the way marketers connect with their cult. By keeping well- informed, chapter marketers can acclimatise to new openings, remain competitive, and insure strategies match with the ever- changing dynamics of the online business.

1. The vital part of Information

- Industry Dynamics

chapter marketing works within the wider environment of the digital marketing assiduity. Staying streamlined on assiduity dynamics is pivotal for understanding the larger forces impacting client geste

, hunt machine algorithms, and the **overall competitive terrain.**

-Technological Advancements

Technology plays a central part in shaping chapter marketing strategies. Keeping abreast of technological advancements, similar as new analytics tools, robotization results, or arising platforms, allows marketers to harness the rearmost tools to enhance their juggernauts.

- Consumer Trends
Consumer geste
is continually evolving,
affected by factors like
changed preferences,
arising trends, and
societal shifts. Staying
informed about
consumer trends allows
chapter marketers to
align their strategies
with the current
requirements and
prospects of their target
followership.

**2. Sources of Information -
Assiduity Publications
and Blogs** Regularly
read assiduity
publications and blogs
devoted to mate
marketing. These spots
give perceptivity into

the rearmost trends, case studies, and stylish practices. Following estimable blogs and publications keeps marketers streamlined about the strategies employed by assiduity leaders.

-   **Webinars and Online Events**

share in webinars and online events held by business experts and associations. Webinars offer a dynamic platform for learning about new technologies, strategies, and success stories straight from professionals in the field. They also give chances for networking and collaboration.

- Podcasts

here to podcasts concentrated on chapter marketing and analogous diligence. Podcasts frequently feature interviews with experts, conversations on current trends, and useful perceptivity. They offer a accessible way to absorb knowledge while on the go.

- Affiliate Networks and Platforms Stay connected with chapter networks and spots. These companies frequently partake updates, adverts , and information about new chapter programs. Regularly checking communication channels within chapter networks ensures marketers are apprehensive of program changes and possibilities.

- Social Media

Follow assiduity leaders, associations, and influencers on social media spots. Social media is a dynamic place where professionals partake perceptivity, news, and conversations about the rearmost happenings in chapter marketing. Engaging in important exchanges on spots like Twitter or LinkedIn keeps marketers in the circle.

3. Monitoring Affiliate Program Changes

- Program adverts

Regularly check for adverts
from chapter programs in which you join. chapter programs may introduce new goods, change commission structures, or update terms and conditions. Being apprehensive of these changes helps marketers to acclimate their strategies consequently.

- Newsletters and Updates

Subscribe to newsletters offered by chapter programs. numerous programs shoot regular updates to their cells, participating information about future elevations, product launches, and changes to the program structure. Newsletters are a direct channel for staying streamlined about program-specific details.

- Affiliate Program Forums

share in forums or discussion groups devoted to chapter marketing and special chapter programs. These forums frequently serve as precious platforms for cells to partake perceptivity, bandy program changes, and seek help. laboriously engaging in these communities gives immediate information.

- Direct Communication

Maintain open contact with chapter program directors. Establishing a direct line of contact allows marketers to admit substantiated updates, seek explanation on program changes, and make connections with the program's support platoon.

4. Adaption to Algorithm Changes - Search Engine Algorithms Hunt machines, especially Google, constantly modernise their algorithms. These updates can impact the visibility of chapter material in hunt results. Staying informed about algorithm changes allows marketers to acclimatize their SEO strategies to insure continued exposure and business.

- **SEO Assiduity Updates**

Follow updates from the SEO assiduity, including changes in stylish practices, algorithm interpretations, and new trends. The SEO geography evolves, and staying informed guarantees that marketers are employing effective optimization strategies.

- Algorithmic Penalties

Be apprehensive of possible algorithmic penalties that may affect chapter websites. Understanding the guidelines set by hunt machines and proactively addressing any issues can help avoid penalties and maintain a strong online presence.

5. Product Launches and Industry Trends

- Product Launch Schedules

Keep track of product launch dates within your niche. Understanding when new goods are set to be released allows marketers to plan their content timetables, produce expectation, and subsidise the excitement girding product launches

- Assiduity Reports and Studies

Stay informed about business reports and studies. These reports frequently show request trends, client preferences, and growth protrusions. penetrating estimable assiduity 1studies provides a macroscopic view of the chapter marketing terrain.

- contender Analysis

Conduct regular contender analysis to

discover what goods or strategies challengers are emphasising. Monitoring challengers' conditioning offers lll into request trends, arising niches, and possible gaps in the **chapter geography.**

- **Networking and Conferences** Attend business conferences and networking events. These gatherings give chances to connect with professionals, learn about forthcoming products, and gain perceptivity from keynote speakers. Conferences offer an immediate look at business trends and inventions.

6.   erecting   a Competitive Edge
-   Innovation   and Experimentation

Foster a spirit of invention and trial within your chapter marketing strategy. Stay open to trying new ideas, platforms, or content formats. Innovation allows marketers to discover unique approaches that can set them piecemeal from rivals.

- nonstop literacy

Commit to ongoing literacy. Enroll in classes, attend shops, or pursue instruments related to chapter marketing and digital marketing in general.

Staying educated about the rearmost strategies and tools adds to professional growth.

- **conforming to Consumer Preferences**
Monitor shifts in consumer preferences and adapt your strategies properly. As consumer habits change, aligning your content and promotional strategies with current preferences ensures that you remain relevant to your target audience.

- **Global Market Trends:**
Consider world market trends and not just local or regional ones. The affiliate marketing landscape is affected by

foreign trends and global consumer behaviors. Being aware of broader trends helps marketers to tap into diverse markets and opportunities.

7. Legal and Regulatory Updates:

- Affiliate Marketing Laws:

Stay informed about affiliate marketing rules and regulations. Legal factors, such as disclosure requirements, vary by jurisdiction. Complying with legal standards guarantees that your affiliate marketing activities are transparent, ethical, and avoid potential legal issues.

- Privacy and Data Protection:

Keep abreast of privacy and data security regulations. Changes in data protection rules, such as GDPR or CCPA, impact how marketers collect, handle, and use consumer data. Adapting to these regulations is important for keeping trust and compliance.

- Ethical Marketing Practices:

Stay updated on ethical marketing techniques. As consumer awareness grows, ethical concerns in marketing become increasingly important. Being aligned with ethical standards not only ensures legal compliance but also helps to building a positive brand reputation.

8. Setting Up Information Channels:
- Customised News Feeds:
Create personalised news feeds using RSS readers or news aggregator apps. Curate sites that provide timely updates on affiliate marketing
, digital marketing, and related sectors. Customized news feeds allow for efficient information consumption.

- **Email Subscriptions:**

Subscribe to email newsletters from business experts, organisations, and platforms. Email subscriptions offer curated content directly to your inbox, ensuring you stay informed without actively seeking updates.

- **Alerts and Notifications:**

Set up alerts and notifications for specific keywords or topics related to affiliate marketing. Automated alerts ensure that you receive instant notifications about breaking news, program changes, or industry trends.

- **Professional Associations:** Join professional groups or communities related to affiliate marketing. These associations often provide newsletters, forums, and exclusive material that keep members informed about industry developments and best practices.

In conclusion, staying updated is not just a practice; it's an attitude that underpins the success of affiliate marketers. By actively seeking information, adopting a culture of continuous learning, and adapting to the ever-evolving digital environment, affiliate marketers position themselves to navigate challenges, leverage new opportunities, and remain at the forefront of the dynamic affiliate marketing industry. As technology, consumer behaviors, and market trends change, the commitment to staying updated ensures that affiliate marketing strategies stay relevant, effective, and set for sustained success over time.

conclusion,

The road to success in chapter marketing is a

testament to the merits of time, fidelity, and thickness. This dynamic realm demands a commitment to ongoing literacy, rigidity, and a loyal focus on furnishing genuine value to your followership. As you navigate the intricate pathways of chapter marketing, keep in mind that late triumphs are rare; rather, success is cultivated through patient trouble and an unvarying commitment to your craft. The foundation of your chapter marketing bid lies in knowing that erecting trust and furnishing authentic value to your followership are consummate. constantly creating material that resonates, informs, and enriches the lives of your followers creates a foundation of credibility. Trust is the currency that promotes lasting connections, and it's these connections that form the bedrock of a successful chapter marketing adventure. tolerance becomes a virtue as you sow the seeds of your sweats. Success in chapter marketing isn't immediate, but rather a gradational process that unfolds over time. It involves enriching your strategies grounded on data- driven perceptivity, conforming to assiduity shifts, and staying attuned to the developing wants and preferences of your followership. Flash back, the incremental progress you make each day adds to the accretive success of your chapter marketing trip. thickness is the cement that holds your sweats together. Whether it's constantly producing high- quality content, nurturing connections with chapter mates, or enriching your approach grounded on analytics, the steady metre of your conduct forms the metre of success. thickness isn't just about keeping a regular advertisement schedule but also about constantly honing your chops, optimising your strategies, and staying married to the long-term vision. As you cut the chapter marketing geography, keep your focus on the value you bring to your community. Your success is naturally tied to the trust you make and the effect you make in the lives of those who engage with your content. Every piece of precious information, every authentic recommendation, and every meaningful commerce adds to the shade of your success. In the world of chapter marketing, income is a derivative of the value you give. It's a reflection of the trust you've earned, the connections you've nurtured, and the applicability of your suggestions. By staying devoted to the core principles of authenticity, thickness, and a genuine fidelity to your followership, you set the stage for sustainable success. So, as you embark on or continue your chapter marketing trip, carry with you the idea that success is a capstone of time- tested principles. Stay devoted, be patient, and constantly strive to give meaningful value. In doing so, you not only pave the way for fiscal earnings but also make a continuing impact on the lives of your followership — a true testament to the substance of success in the world of chapter marketing. **Thanks for reading, hoping to see you at the top.**

www.ingramcontent.com/pod-product-compliance
Lightning Source LLC
Chambersburg PA
CBHW060041260726

48658CB00004B/1141